4/00

Foals

Kelly Doudna

Publishing Company

Published by SandCastle™, an imprint of ABDO Publishing Company, 4940 Viking Drive, Edina, Minnesota 55435.

Printed in the United States.

Photo credits: Kevin Morris/©Corbis, Kit Houghton Photography/Corbis, Neil Miller; Papilio/Corbis, Corel

Library of Congress Cataloging-in-Publication Data

Doudna, Kelly, 1963-
    Foals / Kelly Doudna.
       p. cm. -- (Baby animals)
    Summary: Describes the physical characteristics and behavior of
this common domestic animal.
    ISBN 1-57765-183-9
    1. Foals--Juvenile literature. [1. Horses. 2. Animals-
-Infancy.] I. Title. II. Series: Doudna, Kelly, 1963- Baby
animals.
SF302.D68 1999
636.1'07--DC21   98-21701
                                                      CIP
                                                      AC

The SandCastle concept, content, and reading method have been reviewed and approved by a national advisory board including literacy specialists, librarians, elementary school teachers, early childhood education professionals, and parents.

Let Us Know

After reading the book, SandCastle would like you to tell us your stories about reading. What is your favorite page? Was there something hard that you needed help with? Share the ups and downs of learning to read. We want to hear from you! To get posted on the Abdo Publishing Company Web site, send us email at:

sandcastle@abdopub.com

About SandCastle™
Nonfiction books for the beginning reader

- Basic concepts of phonics are incorporated with integrated language methods of reading instruction. Most words are short, and phrases, letter sounds, and word sounds are repeated.

- Readability is determined by the number of words in each sentence, the number of characters in each word, and word lists based on curriculum frameworks.

- Full-color photography reinforces word meanings and concepts.

- "Words I Can Read" list at the end of each book teaches basic elements of grammar, helps the reader recognize the words in the text, and builds vocabulary.

- Reading levels are indicated by the number of flags on the castle.

Look for more SandCastle books in these three reading levels:

Level 1 (one flag)	**Level 2** (two flags)	**Level 3** (three flags)

Grades Pre-K to K 5 or fewer words per page	**Grades K to 1** 5 to 10 words per page	**Grades 1 to 2** 10 to 15 words per page

A young horse is
a foal.

Foals are tall and
thin.

Foals have long legs.

Foals eat grass.

Horses have long tails.

Foals have short tails.

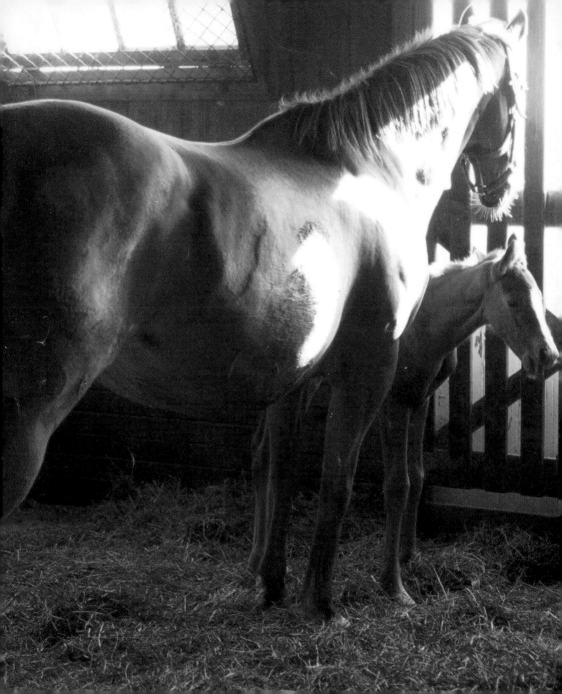

Most foals live on farms.

Some foals live in barns.

This foal runs and plays outside.

This foal runs in
a field.

This foal likes to rest
on the grass.

Some foals are shy.

Can you guess why?

Some foals are not shy.

Are you shy?

Words I Can Read

Nouns

A noun is a person, place, or thing

field (FEELD) p. 15
foal (FOHL) pp. 5, 13, 15, 17
grass (GRASS) pp. 7, 17
horse (HORSS) p. 5

Plural Nouns

A plural noun is more than one
person, place, or thing

barns (BARNZ) p. 11
farms (FARMZ) p. 11
foals (FOHLZ) pp. 5, 7, 9, 11, 19, 21
horses (HORSS-ez) p. 9
legs (LEGZ) p. 7
tails (TAYLZ) p. 9

Verbs

A verb is an action or being word

are (AR) pp. 5, 19, 21
can (KAN) p. 19
eat (EET) p. 7

guess (GESS) p. 19
have (HAV) pp. 7, 9
is (IZ) p. 5
likes (LIKESS) p. 17
live (LIV) p. 11
plays (PLAYZ) p. 13
rest (REST) p. 17
runs (RUHNZ) pp. 13, 15

Adjectives

An adjective describes something

long (LAWNG) pp. 7, 9
most (MOHST) p. 11
short (SHORT) p. 9
shy (SHYE) pp. 19, 21
some (SUHM) pp. 11, 19, 21
tall (TAWL) p. 5
thin (THIN) p. 5
young (YUHNG) p. 5

Sight Words

barn　　　　　**tail**

field